Jon Mogul, editor
Marlene Tosca, art director
Lisa Li and Whitney Richardson, coordinators
David Almeida and Lynton Gardiner, photographers

The Wolfsonian–Florida International University
1001 Washington Ave
Miami Beach, Florida 33139
USA
www.wolfsonian.org

The Wolfsonian receives ongoing support from John S. and James L. Knight Foundation; State of Florida, Department of State, Division of Cultural Affairs and the Florida Council on Arts and Culture; Miami-Dade County Department of Cultural Affairs and the Cultural Affairs Council, the Miami-Dade County Mayor and Board of County Commissioners; and City of Miami Beach, Cultural Affairs Program, Cultural Arts Council.

Cover image (detail)
Lieutenant Costantino Cattoi, *Asiago dopo l'incendio* (Asiago after the Fire), c. 1917

Inside cover image (detail)
Maurice Busset, *Parisiens se rendant aux abris souterrains* (Parisians Rushing into Underground Shelters), 1918

Published by The Wolfsonian–Florida International University, Miami Beach

(c) 2014 Florida International University Board of Trustees

All rights reserved.
No part of this book may be reproduced or utilized in any form or by any means, electronic or mechanical, including photocopying, recording, or by any information or retrieval system, without permission from the copyright holders.

Printed and bound in the United States of America by Shapco
First edition

ISSN 2330-8915

Library of Congress Cataloging-in-Publication Data

Myth and machine : art and aviation in the First World War / Essays by Jon Mogul and Peter Clericuzio. -- First edition.
    pages cm
Issued in connection with an exhibition held Nov. 11, 2014-Apr. 5, 2015, The Wolfsonian, Miami Beach, Florida.
  "No. 2 in a series of publications focused on core themes in the Wolfsonian's collection."
  Includes bibliographical references and index.
  ISBN 978-0-9677359-7-9 (pbk. : alk. paper)
1. World War, 1914-1918--Art and the war. 2. Air warfare in art. 3. World War, 1914-1918--Aerial operations.
I. Mogul, Jonathan, 1963- Art of aerial warfare. II. Clericuzio, Peter. Maurice Busset's modernity. III. Wolfsonian-Florida International University.
  N8260.M87 2014
  704.9'4994044--dc23
                    2014038700

myth+ MACHINE
Art and Aviation in the First World War

Essays by Jon Mogul and Peter Clericuzio

The Wolfsonian
FLORIDA INTERNATIONAL UNIVERSITY

CONTENTS

Foreword 7
Sharon Misdea

The Art of Aerial Warfare 9
Jon Mogul

**Maurice Busset's Modernity:
The Prints of *Paris bombardé*** 23
Peter Clericuzio

Paris bombardé 33
Prints by Maurice Busset

Plates 57

Image captions 89

Foreword

The Wolfsonian–FIU opened to the public on Armistice Day, 1995, at the eleventh hour, on the eleventh day, of the eleventh month. That morning, museum founder Mitchell Wolfson, Jr. dedicated The Wolfsonian to "the path of reconciliation and tolerance," following in the spirit of the 1918 armistice that signaled the end of one of the most destructive and disruptive wars in modern memory.

The First World War was a decidedly modern conflict—one that revealed the horrifying potential of the machine age. The Wolfsonian's collection richly illustrates how visual artists depicted the brutal reality of mechanized warfare as well as the range of strategies they employed to make sense of unimaginable carnage and destruction—from the deployment of new forms of expression to the revival of visual conventions that contained and sanitized the trauma of the war. For us, a century later and generations removed from the war, these works disclose details of the wartime experience that are often eclipsed by retrospective synopsis.

Myth and Machine: Art and Aviation in the First World War, second in a series of publications drawn from The Wolfsonian's collection, considers the artistic expressions of fear and wonder inspired by a new military technology. Jon Mogul's essay, "The Art of Aerial Warfare," is a survey of how artists from several countries conveyed the overwhelming sensory experience of war in the sky, took advantage of aerial perspective to depict terrestrial battle, and celebrated aviators and their exploits. Peter Clericuzio's essay focuses in on a work by French artist Maurice Busset—a portfolio of prints that captures the terror, but also the thrilling spectacle, of the 1918 German air raids on Paris. Both essays illustrate how new armaments such as aircraft became visual icons of war. The publication of this volume coincides with The Wolfsonian's exhibition, *Myth and Machine: The First World War in Visual Culture*, curated by Jon Mogul.

I thank Jon and the talented Wolfsonian staff for their dedication to realizing the book and the exhibition. Recognition is also much due to the generous lenders to the exhibition, whose collections are important elements of the narrative. Finally, on behalf of the staff, let me express my gratitude to Micky Wolfson for his indefatigable efforts to further strengthen The Wolfsonian's collection, which has helped us tell this compelling story. It is in the spirit of his inaugural dedication that we carry forward our commitment to knowledge as the surest foundation of cultural alliance.

Sharon Aponte Misdea
Deputy Director for Collections and Curatorial Affairs

The Art of Aerial Warfare
Jon Mogul

"War pictures of today have no roots in the past." These words appear in the introduction to a catalog, written by American collector and critic A. E. Gallatin, for an exhibition of war art that opened in December 1918 at the American Art Galleries in New York. Artists who wanted to convey the reality of the First World War could not depend on what Gallatin called the "sign-posts" of earlier depictions of battle, whether from ancient times, the Middle Ages, or even the relatively recent Napoleonic Wars.

As an example, Gallatin contrasted the "athletic figures" on the Parthenon frieze with the machine gunners painted by British artist C. R. W. Nevinson who appear to be a "part of the machine"[1]—or, in Nevinson's words, "mere cogs in the mechanism."[2] Indeed, one of the chief challenges faced by artists during the war was how to portray the radical mechanization of warfare and its impact on bodies, psyches, and landscapes.[3]

Among the many machines that figured prominently in the First World War, none was a more magnetic subject for artists than the airplane. During the First World War, forces from the combatant countries took to the skies to conduct reconnaissance, direct artillery fire, bomb targets on the ground, and battle each other in dogfights. Aerial warfare was not a matter for airplanes alone—hot-air balloons and zeppelins also played important roles—but heavier-than-air flying machines had the greatest impact. The modern aviation industry itself was born during the First World War, progressing from what one historian has called "machine shop improvisation" to standardization and mass production over the course of a few years.[4] [fig. 1] By the end of the war, each of the major combatant countries was turning out thousands of airplanes in a year.[5]

Airplanes, more than any other kind of armament, came to symbolize the highly technological and immensely destructive warfare that emerged between 1914 and 1918. As material in

The Wolfsonian's collection makes evident, aerial warfare had a striking cultural resonance across national lines as a source of both fear and wonder, a new vantage from which to see and depict war and its impacts, and an arena for action by a distinctly modern kind of hero.

THE CAPACITY OF AERIAL WARFARE to inflict terrifying destruction became a familiar trope in twentieth-century culture, from *Guernica* to *Slaughterhouse Five* to Nick Ut's famous photograph of Vietnamese victims of a napalm attack. This annihilatory potential was already on the minds of Europeans practically from the birth of modern aviation. H. G. Wells, for example, famously prophesied the doom of civilization as a result of devastation wrought by worldwide aerial war in his 1908 novel *The War in the Air*.[6] While the consequences of the real air war of 1914–18 hardly matched Wells's nightmare scenario, they did little to alleviate the dread that the new machines could provoke. Airplanes appear in the apocalyptic imagery of a series of etchings that Austrian artist Ludwig Hesshaimer (1872–1956) made as illustrations for his poem *Der Weltkrieg: Ein Totentanz* (The World War: A Dance of Death), published in 1921. Rendering the war in terms of the Book of Revelation, Hesshaimer shows airplanes wreaking havoc on the ground in tandem with the Horsemen of the Apocalypse and, together with a tank, joining enormous demons to spit "steel and fire" at miniscule people fleeing across an incinerated landscape.[pl. XVI–XVII]

While Hesshaimer's airplanes figure in an allegory that universalizes their meaning as agents of biblical destruction, French artist Maurice Busset (1879–1936) documented a particular episode of the air war—a series of German nighttime bombing raids on Paris in 1918—in the print portfolio *Paris bombardé* (Paris Bombarded), most likely published in 1919. Busset, who, like Hesshaimer, was an official war artist, made several prints that show the raids from the perspective of a person on the street, looking across the city from an elevated point or viewing the chaotic aftermath of a bomb hit.[pl. XIV–XV] But Busset also recorded the battle in the air. In two especially

fig. 1 *Women Welding Water Jackets on Liberty Engine Cylinders*, c. 1917

vivid prints, he presented midair perspectives on the raids—one from just above a squadron of the enemy's Gotha bombers, the other from just below a French Breguet fighter.[pl. V, VII] These scenes have a phantasmagoric quality stemming from the blues and purples of the night skies, pierced by diagonal rays of searchlights and illuminated by bursts of anti-aircraft shells, as well as from the sinuous form of the Seine far below and the reptilian, scale-like pattern on the wings of the bombers. In creating a visual record of impressions and experiences that could scarcely have been imagined by people living just a generation earlier, Busset created scenes that mingle terror and beauty.

While Busset's *Paris bombardé* portrays air combat as dazzling spectacle, C. R. W. Nevinson (1889–1946) sought to convey the sensory impact of flight itself. In the early years of the war, Nevinson made his reputation with trenchant renderings—some owing a debt to Futurism—of mechanized warfare, including several paintings about military aviation.[7] In 1917 he took a position as an official war artist for the British Ministry of Information. Among the works he made in that capacity is a series of six lithographs titled *Building Aircraft*.[8] Three of these works stay true to that title,[pl. XVIII–XX] while the other three shift attention to flight itself. *Swooping Down on*

11

a Taube shows a British biplane diving in pursuit of a German Taube ("pigeon" or "dove," so named for the birdlike form of its wings) far below.[pl. XXI] The plane plunges through a sky that Nevinson depicts as a dynamic and disorienting space, with shafts of light slashing at different angles across the picture plane, billowing clouds, and a jagged play of light and dark forming an ambiguous pattern in the distance.

It is unlikely that Nevinson would have viewed such a chase from the elevated perspective suggested here, but he did log time in the air in 1917 on practice runs in Britain and reconnaissance flights over France, which may have been the basis for the other two prints in this series. *Banking at 4,000 Feet* puts the viewer in the rear seat of an aircraft as it wheels above a patchwork of fields and roads.[pl. XXII] The hand gripping the rail, the sense of gravitational force generated by the plane's banking action (pushing the perspective slightly out of line with the fuselage, as if the viewer's head, like the pilot's, has been forced down and to the right), the great distance to the ground below, and the vastness of sky and earth perceptible at this great height, all suggest the astonishment and terror that flight induced, even in relatively peaceful circumstances. *In the Air*, though the least dynamic image in the series, offers that same perception of vastness and great depth.[pl. XXIII]

AVIATION WAS MORE THAN an inviting subject for artists; it also offered a view of battle on earth from highly revealing vantage points. War on the ground, particularly on the Western Front, presented unfamiliar challenges for artists. On a battlefield where visibility was an invitation to death, infantrymen spent the better part of their time sheltered in trenches, dugouts, or shell craters, making them largely invisible to an artist (or a machine-gunner) on the earth's surface. An aerial perspective, by contrast, offered visual information that enabled artists to convey a rich account of the battleground.

An etching by André Devambez (1867–1944), *Les trous d'obus* (The Shell Holes), shows a scene of battle in France from the perspective of a low-flying aircraft.[pl. XXIV] In several prewar works, Devambez had captured the ethereal grace of flying machines and the fascination they provoked among the French public.[9] During the war, while deployed in France's camouflage service, he depicted a battlefield from practically overhead, showing a barren, blasted landscape marked by huge shell craters. In the more distant craters, infantrymen sit and stand rather casually, suggesting they are not in immediate danger. In the large crater in the foreground, however, the soldiers seem about to scramble out and retreat to safer shelter. In between is one soldier who appears to be crawling across the ground, crouched in a slight depression in the earth with his back to the viewer. Devambez uses the aerial view to map how war has reshaped the earth's surface and to emphasize the extreme vulnerability of soldiers on that lethal terrain.[10]

What aerial views, even low ones, offer in terms of breadth of vision over the battlefield, they lose in terms of the ability to portray the qualities and experiences of people. In Devambez's scene, soldiers huddle together and blend into the landscape. Their forms are visible, but their faces are not, and the viewer learns nothing about them as individuals. Viewed from a higher altitude, they become even less distinct. A lithograph by Anselmo Bucci (1887–1955), part of a series based on sketches he made while observing Italian soldiers and sailors during a number of campaigns in 1918, uses two registers to dramatize the visual divide between sky and earth. [pl. XXV] The image at the bottom brings the viewer into a trench, in close quarters with soldiers who gaze up at an unseen object in the sky. A scribbled note at the lower right tells what they have sighted: *nostri aeroplani* [our airplanes]. The top half of the print gives an aerial perspective over a rural landscape where several structures, roads, and a waterway are recognizable, but people are merely suggested by a dozen or so short dark marks.
If airplanes are easy to spot from below, those in the trenches are barely, if at all, discernible to the aviator high above.

People on the ground vanish altogether when viewed from altitudes of several thousand feet or higher typically reached by First World War reconnaissance flights. The chief visual records of the war from these heights are the hundreds of thousands of photographs shot by the air services of the combatant countries. Military planners in Germany, France, and Britain began experimenting with photography from airplanes in the years before the start of the conflict, and Captain Carlo Piazza shot aerial photos over Libya during military operations in Italy's war with Turkey in 1911–12.[11] Aerial reconnaissance photography played a role in early campaigns on the Western and Eastern Fronts in 1914, spurring improvements in both aviation and camera technology and closer operational integration of air fleets with ground and naval forces. Armies began using mobile laboratories to develop each day's photographs. Camouflage services used decoys and coverings to confound interpretation of these images. Reconnaissance services then responded by using semi-automated cameras to produce series of closely spaced, precisely timed exposures—the basis for prints that could be viewed in pairs through a stereoscope, enabling interpreters to discern depth and elevation in the landscape.[12]

Aerial photography also informed the way the public viewed the conflict. During the war, aerial photographs appeared in such popular periodicals as the *Mid-Week Pictorial* of the *New York Times*, *L'Illustration*, the *Illustrated London News*, and *L'Illustrazione Italiana*.[fig. 2] Similar photographs were also included in sets of stereoscopic cards, among shots of infantry charges, tanks crushing barbed wire, and naval battles, issued by British and American publishers during and after the war. After 1918, aerial reconnaissance photographs acquired aesthetic caché—exemplified by Edward Steichen's gift of a group of such photographs to the Museum of Modern Art—thanks to their formal consonance with abstraction (particularly Cubism) in painting.[13]

It was a Rome-based art publisher that issued *Visione alata della guerra d'Italia* (Winged Vision of Italy's War) shortly after the war, an album of Italian aerial reconnaissance photographs compiled by Lieutentant Costantino Cattoi (1894–1975),

fig. 2 *Cima Dodici*, 1917

who had flown missions as an aerial observer during the war. The poetic title is one indication that the album was to be received not just as documentation of Italy's struggle against Austria-Hungary, but also as an object meant for aesthetic appreciation; another indication was the inclusion of several art prints separating the groups of photographs.[pl. XXVI] The photographs are indeed striking in formal terms. Many feature the dramatic play of light and shadow on alpine ridges.[pl. XXVII] Others reveal the street patterns of towns or the contours of the Palmanova citadel.[pl. XXVIII] In one, branches of the Piave River form what looks like an abstract pattern against a black landscape.[pl. XXIX] Most arresting, however, is how the photographs register the impact of war on the natural landscape and the built environment. They reveal the surface of Mount Asolone carved up by an intricate system of trenches;[pl. XXX]

15

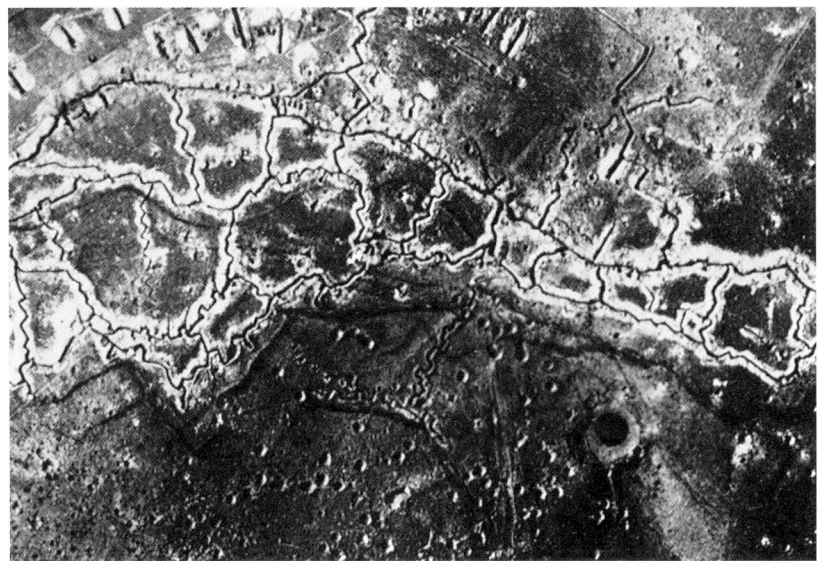

the foundations of buildings in Asiago exposed after a fire that razed the town;[pl. XXXI] plumes of smoke from a bombardment on Mount Zebbio;[pl. XXXII] and the remains of a wrecked bridge over the Piave.[pl. XXXIII] In many of the photographs, close scrutiny reveals dozens or hundreds of shell craters in the landscape,[fig. 3] but no people, living or dead.[14]

NEAR THE END OF HIS ALBUM, Cattoi included four photographs that record a famous exploit by the writer and aviator Gabriele D'Annunzio. On August 9, 1918, a squadron of nine Italian planes took off from Padua and crossed the Alps, eventually reaching Vienna, where the Italians dropped hundreds of thousands of patriotic leaflets for the Viennese (at least those who knew Italian) to read.[pl. XXXIV] One photograph shows D'Annunzio's airplane[15] from directly overhead.[pl. XXXV] Another shows the leaflets cascading down onto the city.[pl. XXXVI] While most of the images in *Visione alata* are reconnaissance photographs, those concerning D'Annunzio were intended as publicity. Two of them had already been published immediately after the squadron's flight in an extended feature that appeared in the August 18, 1918, issue of *L'Illustrazione Italiana*, with a soft-focus portrait of the romantic figure of D'Annunzio on the cover. [fig. 4]

fig. 3 *Monte Grappa—Le trincee dell'Asolone (Mount Grappa—The Trenches of Asalone), c. 1917 (detail)*

D'Annunzio was just one of many aviators to emerge as popular heroes from the First World War—their adventures in the air reported and embellished by publicity machines on the ground. Historians agree about the reasons for the glorification of flyers, particularly the "aces" who dueled each other in dogfights. In part, this fascination was simply an extension of pre-war culture, in which the advent of heavier-than-air flying machines was greeted in poetry and prose as the dawn of a new era in human achievement and consciousness. During these years, Wilbur Wright became a figure (at least in France) of open veneration, and the risky pursuit of speed, range, and altitude records by wealthy and daring young men captivated the public.[16] After 1914, the flying ace filled what Stefan Goebel has called a "compensatory function" in the context of a war that fit very poorly with notions of honorable, manly combat.[17] Earth-bound soldiers waited in trenches only to face death and maiming from such impersonal forces as artillery shells launched from miles away, a spray of bullets from a machine gun, or dysentery and other diseases. In the sky, by contrast, airmen fighting one-on-one duels seemed part modern sportsmen, part chivalric knights, their identity reinforced by the fact that most of them came from the upper classes of society.[18] The press kept score of the enemy aircraft shot down by individual aces and gave detailed accounts of

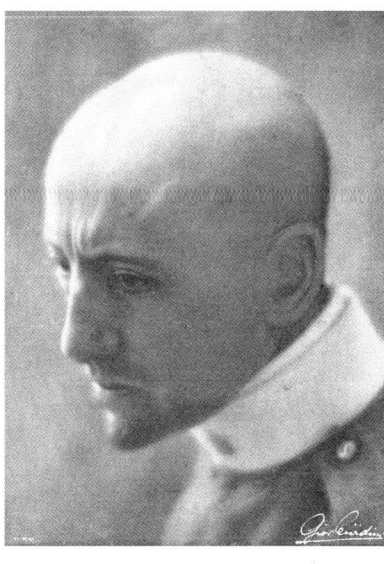

fig. 4 Photograph of Gabriele D'Annunzo, 1918
fig. 5 Giuseppe Palanti, *Il tragico eroico volo del Capitano Salomone* (The Tragic Heroic Flight of Captain Salomone), 1916

dogfights, which were also popular subjects for artists and illustrators.[19] [fig. 5; pl. XXXVII] Writers painted the aces themselves in rhapsodic terms: the French aviator Georges Guynemer's biographer compared him to the legendary French hero Roland, calling him the "last of the knights-errant and the first of the knights of the air," while a poet referred to him as a "young god."[20] Eddie Rickenbacker (United States), Manfred von Richthofen (Germany), "Mick" Mannock (Great Britain), and Francesco Baracca (Italy), among others, similarly became figures of adulation during the war.

This adulation took different visual forms, emphasizing different features of the ace's nature. A series of cover portraits in the German magazine *Wachtfeuer* celebrated that country's aces, each shown in dress uniform, directing a steely gaze to the side or straight at the viewer. [figs. 6–7] A portfolio of woodcuts from 1917 by Victor-Emile Descaves (1899–1959) portrays five of the most famous French airmen: Jean Navarre, Charles Nungesser, Georges Guynemer, Alfred Heurteaux, and René Dorme. [pl. XXXVIII–XLII] Each poses in uniform, dwarfing the aircraft on the ground or in the sky that appear in the background. The naïve effect of these prints, achieved with solid color fields and minimally modeled figures outlined in black, recalls the tradition of *images d'Epinal*, inexpensive woodblock broadsides produced since early modern times in eastern France.[21] Descaves's portraits thus present the flying aces as folkloric figures whose deeds were already the stuff of popular legend. At the same time, their nonchalant poses and their mastery of flying machines identify them as modern men. As with the portraits on the *Wachtfeuer* covers, there is a rigid consistency in the conventions of representation of these airmen, as if they were not just a collection of individuals, but a special breed.

The near identity between the aviator and his flying machine was among the most common tropes of early aviation culture. Even as the aviator controlled the machine, he became machine-like himself, acquiring, in the words of the German

writer Ernst Jünger, "brains of steel."[22] This identity was strong enough that the airplane often functioned as a visual metonym for the airman at the controls. A photograph by the Hungarian aviator János Kugler—part of an album of shots taken by Hungarian troops and issued by the newspaper *Az Érdekes Újság* during the war—makes a dramatically silhouetted monoplane stand in for the almost invisible "Hero of the air," as the image is captioned.[pl. XLIII] The same is true in two German posters designed by Julius Gipkens (1883–1968) for a charity that gave assistance to aviators and their families. In Gipkens's posters the "heroic" and "brave" airmen are barely distinguishable from the machines they are piloting.[pl. XLIV–XLV]

The death rate among airmen was staggering—about one in three British combat pilots were killed in action during the war, for example[23]—and an aviator's death offered an especially powerful opportunity for mythmaking. "His is an ascending death, a veritable flying away," is how one French writer memorialized Guynemer after he was shot down in autumn 1917.[24] A similar rhetoric of ascendance characterized representations of Richthofen, Germany's "Red Baron," after his death in April 1918. The cover of *Wachtfeuer* by Fritz Preiss

figs. 6–7 W. Jordan, Portrait of Manfred von Richthofen, 1917, and Portrait of Rudolf von Eschwege, 1918

19

shows a nude Richtohfen rising into the light on the wing of a Prussian eagle.[pl. XLVI] In the humor magazine *Lustige Blätter*, an illustration by W. A. Wellner (1859–1939) depicts a kind of Norse *Pietà*, as two infantrymen have pulled the dead aviator's body from his wrecked aircraft and are passing him into the arms of a Valkyrie, who will remove him from the battlefield and bear him to Valhalla on her white horse.[pl. XLVII]

THE ATTENTION THAT FLYING ACES like Richthofen received was out of proportion with their importance. The same could be said of aviation in general: it was far from decisive as a military factor in the war, but nonetheless had compelling appeal as an art subject. This essay has identified a number of tendencies evident in depictions of aerial warfare by artists on both sides of the conflict. Flying machines lifted artists out of the squalor and tedium of mechanized warfare on the ground. Aviation offered opportunities to represent the war as a sublime spectacle and to command an entirely novel perspective on the battlefield. The air war seemed a cleaner, more heroic conflict than the ground war, and one much more suitable for the creation of myths. Even while celebrating daring exploits in the sky, however, artists during the First World War also got an early glimpse of the damage that air power could do to people on the ground, damage that would increase exponentially in the century to come.

I would like to thank Matthew Abess, Silvia Barisione, Peter Clericuzio, Jessica Kennedy, Lisa Li, and Marta Zarzycka for their comments on earlier drafts. In addition, Peter Clericuzio and Jordan Malfoy contributed invaluable research.

1. A. E. Gallatin, "Introduction," in *Allied War Salon* (New York: American Art Galleries, 1918), 1.

2. Quoted in Samuel Hynes, *A War Imagined: The First World War and English Culture* (New York: Atheneum, 1991), 162.

3. Ibid., 107–8, 164.

4. Dennis E. Showalter, "Mass Warfare and the Impact of Technology," in Roger Chickering and Stig Förster, eds., *Great War, Total War* (Cambridge: Cambridge University Press, 2000), 84.

5. Martin Van Creveld, "World War I and the Revolution in Logistics," in Chickering and Förster, eds., *Great War, Total War*, 66. Britain, for example, manufactured 200 aircraft in 1914; by 1918 that number had leaped to 32,000.

6. Wells's novel was serialized in 1907. For a description of prefigurations of air war in works by the German writer Rudolf Martin and the French Emile Driant, see Robert Wohl, *A Passion for Wings: Aviation and the Western Imagination, 1907–1918* (New Haven: Yale University Press, 1994), 77–89.

7. Michael J. K. Walsh, "'This Tumult in the Clouds': C. R. W. Nevinson and the Development of the 'Airscape,'" *British Art Journal* 5, 1 (Spring/Summer 2004), 82–83. Jonathan Black, "A Curious, Cold Intensity: C. R. W. Nevinson as War Artist, 1914–1918," in *C. R. W. Nevinson: The Twentieth Century* (London: Merrell Holberton, 1999), 33–35.

8. *Building Aircraft* was part of a series of print portfolios, *The Great War: Britain's Efforts and Ideals*, with contributions by more than a dozen British artists on a variety of subjects.

9. Michel Ménégoz, A*ndré Devambez (1867–1944): presentation d'une donation* (Beauvais: Musée départemental de l'Oise, 1988), 47, 54–56.

10. This same sense of vulnerability is conveyed in a low-altitude photograph of a battlefield in which French soldiers shelter in individual holes they had dug during an advance, published in the August 31, 1918, issue of *Illustrated London News*. See Paula Amad, "From God's-eye to Camera-eye: Aerial Photography's Post-humanist and Neo-humanist Visions of the World," *History of Photography* 36, no. 1 (February 2012), 77.

11. Terrance J. Finnegan, *Shooting the Front: Allied Aerial Reconnaissance and Photographic Interpretation on the Western Front—World War I* (Washington: National Defense Intelligence Press, 2006), 8–12; Richard P. Hallion, *Taking Flight: Inventing the Aerial Age from Antiquity through the First World War* (Oxford: Oxford University Press, 2003), 314.

12. Finnegan, *Shooting the Front*, 15–38, 41-42; Amad, 69; Paul K. Saint-Amour, "Modernist Reconnaissance," *Modernism/Modernity* 10, no. 2 (2003): 358–59.

13. See Patricia Johnson, *Real Fantasies: Edward Steichen's Advertising Photographs* (Berkeley: University of California Press, 1997), 57–58; Saint-Amour, 349–52; Stephen Kern, *The Culture of Time and Space, 1880–1918* (Cambridge: Harvard University Press, 1983; 2003), 245.

14. On the impersonality of the aerial perspective and its implications, both dystopian and utopian, see Amad, 69–72; and Bern Huppauf, "Experiences of Modern Warfare and the Crisis of Representation," *New German Critique* 59 (Spring–Summer 1993), 56–59.

15. D'Annunzio himself was a passenger on this flight.

16. Wohl, 23–29, 125–33.

17. Stefan Goebel, *The Great War and Medieval Memory* (Cambridge: Cambridge University Press, 2007), 227.

18. Wohl, 203–36, 282; Martin Van Creveld, *Technology and War from 2000 B.C. to the Present* (New York: The Free Press, 1989), 188.

19. Linda Raine Robinson, *The Dream of Civilized Warfare: World War I Flying Aces and the American Imagination* (Minneapolis: University of Minnesota Press, 2003), 277, 368; Bernard Wilkin, "Aviation and Propaganda in France during the First World War," *French History* 28, no. 1 (2014), 48.

20. Wohl, 235–36.

21. Kenneth E. Silver, *Esprit de Corps: The Art of the Parisian Avant-Garde and the First World War, 1914–1925* (Princeton: Princeton University Press, 1989), 38–41.

22. Quoted in Peter Fritzsche, "Machine Dreams: Airmindedness and the Reinvention of Germany," *American Historical Review* 98, no. 3 (June 1993), 693.

23. Robinson, 106.

24. Wohl, 235.

Maurice Busset's Modernity: The Prints of *Paris bombardé*
Peter Clericuzio

The luminous beams coming from all the peripheral forts weave a hallucinatory vault above the city in a magical glow; a terrible phantasmagoria, night of modern legend, mysterious and silvery blue, where the giant vultures whirl under the shattered sky...

What Eastern storyteller dared to evoke you, so that on this moonlit night you appear to me on our French soil: pulsating, fantastic Night of War!

—Maurice Busset, "Les Gothas," from *Paris bombardé*[1]

The question of how to depict the new and terrifying phenomenon of aerial warfare faced everyone who chronicled the First World War firsthand: journalists, soldiers, government officials, photographers, and, especially, war artists. The French artist Maurice Busset confronted this challenge in a number of works, including *Paris bombardé* (c. 1919),[2] a portfolio of thirteen colored woodcuts and two etchings[pl. I-II] concerning the raids on the French capital by the German air force during the first half of 1918. Although the print techniques Busset used to depict the events of modern aerial warfare had been well established for centuries, the visual strategies he employed in the portfolio allude quite overtly to the mechanical production of images, particularly photography. It is Busset's negotiation of the balance between traditional and modern image-making technologies that makes his portrayal of the events in *Paris bombardé* so striking.

BUSSET WAS NOT AN ARTIST whom one would expect to produce salient depictions of warfare. Born in 1879 in Clermont–Ferrand, in the Auvergne region of central France, he trained as an academic painter with Jean-Léon Gérome in Paris, and simultaneously learned the techniques of woodblock printing. Busset spent most of his career as a painter of his native region, but in 1914 he was mobilized as part of the French air force (Aéronautique Militaire, then a branch of the French Army),

fig. 1 *Les bombardements aériens de Paris en 1918* (The Aerial Bombardments of Paris in 1918)

becoming a warrant officer, above the ranks of enlisted men. Busset was fascinated by flight and continued sketching while in the army. He was hired as a military painter for the French Museum of Aviation (Musée de l'Aéronautique, now the Musée de l'Air et de l'Espace) upon its creation in 1919, though he soon abandoned aviation subjects and returned permanently to Clermont–Ferrand. There, he took a job as a professor of drawing at the local Ecole des Beaux-Arts. Regional press coverage of his work during the 1920s allowed Busset to obtain a curatorial post at the municipal museum of fine arts, and eventually conferred upon him the status of a local celebrity during his lifetime.[3]

THE AIR RAIDS portrayed in *Paris bombardé* brought the battle-front to the civilian sphere and constituted some of the most harrowing wartime experiences for Parisians.[figs. 1–2] The bombings formed part of the Germans' Spring Offensive of 1918, during which they advanced to within seventy-five miles of Paris. Lasting for five months, from late January through the end of June, the bombings were the first to target Paris since January 1916. They were also the deadliest, claiming 241 lives (as opposed to thirty-four in all previous raids on the capital combined) and leaving hundreds more wounded. The 1918 attacks were the most vigorous of the war, employing modern military technology, such as the long-range artillery guns nicknamed "Big Berthas" that could reach Paris from the German lines, and the Gotha G.V bombers developed in 1917–18 that boasted a seventy-eight-foot wingspan and a carrying capacity for 800 pounds of bombs.[4] These planes exceeded the wingspans of their French counterparts, also seen in Busset's plates—the 1915 Breguet Bre. 5/6/12 fighters and bombers—by more than twenty feet, though the French had re-equipped them with more powerful machine guns and a searchlight by 1918.[5] [pl. V, VII]

Throughout the raids, French reports detailed the stoicism and valor of civilian victims and survivors; predictably, anti-German vitriol reached a fever pitch, with calls for retaliatory air attacks to be launched against defenseless German cities.[6] Air attacks on Paris stopped once the Allies stalled the German offensive in July 1918 with the sustained counterattack that ultimately ended the war.

PARIS BOMBARDÉ is a rather personal account of Busset's experience during the conflict, despite his refusal to use the text to insert himself into the events described. Busset's ability to move between the military and civilian spheres permitted him to effectively capture multiple perspectives during the raids. In some views, he seems to be a journalist standing a few paces

fig. 2 *Parigi: La sala di un asilo infantile colpita dal cannone tedesco che bombarda la città* (Paris: The Room of a Kindergarten Struck by German Cannons that Bombarded the City), c. 1918

25

away from a burning building that has just been hit by a bomb, lighting up the otherwise dark city streets,[pl. XV] while in others, he appears to be scurrying into the Métro with his fellow citizens to escape the aerial bombardment.[pl. VII] Most significantly, he sometimes finds himself with the pilots and gunners in the midst of combat.[pl. XIV] But unlike other French war artists, such as André Devambez, whose extensive time as an aviator is well documented,[7] Busset's firsthand experience with flight is poorly understood; indeed, there appears to be no source that can confirm whether he flew in an airplane before or during the conflict. The plates in *Paris bombardé* provide no resolution to this question, though a sister woodcut portfolio that Busset produced in 1919, *En avion: vols et combats* (In a Plane: Flights and Fights), a paean to French and other Entente aviators, provides such detailed descriptions of flying in battle that it becomes difficult to believe that Busset did not go up in a plane during the war.[8]

Busset was far from the only French wartime artist working with woodcuts, especially since metal for print media was in short supply.[9] Several features of Busset's woodcuts disclose that he cultivated a strong relationship with photography, which by this point had become a standard means of documenting current events. Though not a new process, having been introduced onto the battlefield decades earlier during the American Civil War, photography remained the fastest—and most technologically advanced—means of producing images. Used extensively in aerial reconnaissance from August 1914 onward, photography became the primary way the war was documented from above. The Breguet aircraft depicted in Busset's prints were even originally used for these purposes before being converted for use as fighters.[10]

Woodcuts such as *Les Gothas*,[pl. V] wherein the viewer is imagined as being in a plane and looking down to the ground or toward another aircraft, clearly reference the use of the photographic medium. Several of Busset's images—*Avion canon de la défense en vol sur la cité* (Armed Defense Airplane in Flight over the City),[pl. VIII] for example—are cropped to omit parts of key elements like bodies of planes or the upper levels of buildings, implying that Busset was either working from photographs or intending to recreate the framed action of an aerial snapshot of combat. All of Busset's disseminated wartime images appeared after the armistice in publications identifying him as a military painter for the Musée de l'Aéronautique, which itself was founded only after the cessation of fighting. It is probable, then, that Busset could have been working primarily from photographs in the museum's collection or from those he himself may have taken in flight.

Yet Busset seems to be trying to further enhance the experience of photography by the way he colors his woodcuts in very vivid hues. The turquoise, indigo, and orange tones of *Avion canon de la défense en vol sur la cité*[pl. VIII] are rather fantastical if the print's perspective was borrowed from a photograph or even Busset's own observations of action at ten o'clock on an evening in late January.[11] The scene would have been much darker than Busset's woodcut suggests, and the elements of the composition would have appeared much more shadowy and indistinct to a firsthand observer, if they were visible at all. Not even a viewer situated in the thick of the action in an airplane, as implied in *Les Gothas,*[pl. V] would have noticed the details of the mottled metal skin of the German bombers; nor would the ground itself be illuminated enough to produce a sea-green hue. Busset's intensity of color is, however, reminiscent of the expensive (and rare) autochrome photography that had just been developed and was being put to use with stunning results through the efforts of the industrialist Albert Kahn at this same time, and particularly around Paris.[12] It is likely that Busset saw the advent of modern color photography as direct competition for the vivid hues of traditional painting and printmaking, much the way many of his contemporaries (notably the artists of the German Werkbund) saw the machine as a threat to the individuality of the creator.[13] Busset's license to enhance the hues—and thus the dramatic effect of his depictions—in a way that not even color photography could attain thus hints at this struggle between the mechanical and the artist's hand, and subtly argues for the continued importance of craft in the face of this competition.

Busset's rendering choices, such as the strong black outline of forms, are in part due to the nature of the traditional medium of woodblock prints—which lend themselves to thick, flattened, blocky regions—but they also reveal his awareness of trends in modern art outside photography. The emphasis on flat planes of color, the thick outlines of individual elements, and the juxtaposition of subtle shades of the same color—such as in *La saucisse du Luxembourg* (The Observation Balloon of Luxembourg Garden) [pl. XIII]—recalls the popular work of French Art Nouveau graphic artists like Henri de Toulouse-Lautrec, Théophile Steinlen, and Alfons Mucha (a relationship underscored directly in the plates where Busset depicts Hector Guimard's Parisian Métro entrances).[14] Similarly, these aspects of Busset's work reference the colors of Japanese woodblock prints, which had long been circulating among French enthusiasts. Finally, some of Busset's exaggerated hues—the oranges, reds, pinks, yellows, and browns—suggest his familiarity with Fauvist or Expressionist work in both France and Germany during the 1910s by artists like Wassily Kandinsky, Paul Klee, André Dérain, Robert Delaunay, Sonia Delaunay-Terk, Lionel Feininger, and André Devambez himself.[15]

The design of the portfolio is no less important for its relationship to photography and the latter's far-reaching cultural imprint. Each of Busset's colored images is framed in a well-defined panel with rounded corners, reminiscent of cutout mattes allotted to photographs in a personal album compiled by its owner; thus the prints appear like snapshots taken by a firsthand witness to the events. Likewise, the accompanying text is less a description of what is being depicted than a poetic jotting down of the sights, smells, and sounds of the action. It is like an impression recorded in the immediate aftermath, such as a diary entry—a correlation reinforced by

fig. 3 Maurice Busset, *L'héroisme des soldats de l'air* (The Heroism of the Soldiers in the Air), c. 1919

the dating of each text as one might in a personal journal. There is, therefore, a rawness to the description of these events, not unlike the way a soldier might recount his thoughts of an engagement during a subsequent moment of reflection. The roughness and paucity of the wording suggest that each person who owned a copy was meant to feel a sense of ownership of the experience of having personally lived through the bombardment. The emphasis is on the power of the imagery to fix the vividness of those memories.

Such a reading of *Paris bombardé* is reinforced when one contrasts the construction of this set with Busset's contemporaneous volume *En avion: vols et combats*, which reads like an official history, perhaps one commissioned by the Musée de l'Aéronautique, with short essays in gold print retelling exploits of individual flying aces in precise narrative prose, often supported by statistics. [fig. 3] The title of each essay appears in large capital letters, and the texts are adorned with stylized helmets and other war equipment. *En avion*'s woodcuts, while stylistically similar to those of *Paris bombardé*, appear ambiguous and contrived—indeed, most of them require captions to clarify the scenes—and their basis in photography seems unlikely.[pl. XLVIII] As monochrome prints tinted with only one other hue, they produce a less dynamic visual effect than the multicolored plates of *Paris bombardé*. The primacy in *En avion* lies with the factual text, not the images, making it a less poignant memento of the war.

MANY PARISIANS may have seen the aftermath of the German air attacks of 1918: the rubble, the fiery and smoking ruins of buildings, and even images of victims. But capturing the vivid, fleeting terror spawned by modern technology that only a few had experienced firsthand was a challenge for Busset to solve. Produced in a run of three hundred copies, *Paris bombardé* serves as a reminder of the desperation felt by the capital's citizens during the most harrowing part of the war, and may have been intended to serve as an artistic photo album for those who were present at the events depicted. As an artist, Busset could not escape what technology had done to transform modern life. He therefore co-opted it with remarkable results.

I would like to thank all of those who commented on earlier drafts of this essay and provided useful feedback, particularly Jon Mogul, Matthew Abess, and Cathy Byrd.

1. All translations by the author, unless noted otherwise.

2. No definitive publication date has been established, although the latest events depicted in Busset's portfolio are those of July 14, 1919. Its preface was written by General Pierre Auguste Roques, who died on February 26, 1920, but the portfolio contains no reference to Roques's death; thus it seems most likely that *Paris bombardé* appeared in print during the latter half of 1919.

3. See "Quelques livres d'étrennes," in *Le correspondent* 277 (December 10, 1919): 959; and Henri Pourrat, "L'Ile au trésor," in *L'Auvergne littéraire* 2, no. 17 (May 1, 1925): 2–10.

4. Susan Grayzel, "'The Souls of Soldiers': Civilians Under Fire in First World War France," *Journal of Modern History* 78 (September 2006): 596, 606; also "Big German Battleplane Splendidly Designed," in *Popular Mechanics* 28, no. 4 (October 1917): 513.

5. On these, see John Howard Morrow, Jr., *The Great War in the Air: Military Aviation from 1909 to 1921* (Washington, DC: Smithsonian Institution Press, 1993), 143–44, 205, 220–21, 232, and 281–96; idem., *German Air Power in World War I* (Lincoln: University of Nebraska Press, 1982), 116–17; Lee Kennett, *The First Air War, 1914–1918* (New York: Free Press, 1991), 213–16; and Emmanuel Breguet and Nicolas Bardou, *Breguet: un siècle d'aviation* (Toulouse: Privat, 2012), 36–43.

6. Grayzel, 607–13.

7. For Devambez, see Michel Ménégoz, André Devambez: (1867–1944): *presentation d'une donation* (Beauvais: Musée Départemental de l'Oise, 1988); and *Cahiers d'études ct dc recherches du musée de l'Armée* 1 (2000): Peindre de la Grande Guerre 1914–1918: *Actes du symposium de l'AMAM*, 42–43.

8. Busset, *En avion: vols et combats: estampes et récits de la Grande Guerre* (Paris: Librairie Delagrave, 1919). One review of *En avion* called it "the tribute of a fighting airman to the memory of his intrepid comrades of the French Flying Corps….[H]is prints recording some of their daring exploits bear the unmistakable impress of actuality," as "expressions of an artist who has had personal experience of aerial warfare." See "Reviews," in *The International Studio* 70, no. 279 (May 1920): 80. I have not consulted any French government records documenting Busset's military service.

9. See Jon Mogul's essay in this volume. Devambez, Charles Barclay de Tholey, Hermann-Paul, Robert Bonfils, and Victor-Emile Descaves all produced prints of war subjects during the conflict.

10. Breguet and Bardou, 38.

11. As described in the accompanying text, "Sous les Bombes," the scene concerns the events of January 30, 1918.

12. On autochromes, consult John Wood, *The Art of the Autochrome: The Birth of Color Photography* (Iowa City: University of Iowa Press, 1993); *Paris 1910–1931: au travers des autochromes et des films de la Photothèque-cinémathèque* Albert Kahn (Paris: Musée Carnavalet, 1982); and David Okefuena, *The Wonderful World of Albert Kahn: Colour Photographs from a Lost Age* (London: BBC, 2008).

13. On the controversy between craft and machine within the German Werkbund, see John Maciuika, *Before the Bauhaus: Architecture and Politics in Germany 1890–1920* (Cambridge, UK: Cambridge University Press, 2005) 264–82; and Frederic Schwartz, *Design Theory & Mass Culture Before the First World War* (New Haven: Yale University Press, 1996), 147–63.

14. On these artists, see Stephen J. Eskilson, *Graphic Design: A New History*, 2nd ed. (New Haven: Yale University Press, 2012), 59–70; and Gabrièle Fahr-Becker, *Art Nouveau* (Cologne: Könemann, 2004), 75–85, 90–93, 100–103.

15. For parallel developments in French art during this period, see Kenneth Silver, *Esprit de Corps: The Art of the Parisian Avant-Garde and the First World War, 1914–1925* (Princeton: Princeton University Press, 1989).

MAURICE BUSSET'S *Paris bombardé* is a series of recollections of the large-scale bombardment of the French capital during the first six months of 1918 by the invading Germans. The portfolio consists of two etchings and thirteen woodcuts interleaved with one-page texts—not reproduced in the following plates—that record Busset's momentary impressions of the accompanying scenes. The prints depict Parisians' harrowing experiences during the most serious episodes of violence inflicted upon the city during the First World War. At the same time, they demonstrate Busset's fascination and familiarity with the new phenomenon of aerial warfare.

Most of the prints are dated 1918, but Busset did not complete the series until 1919, and the portfolio was probably published near the end of that year.

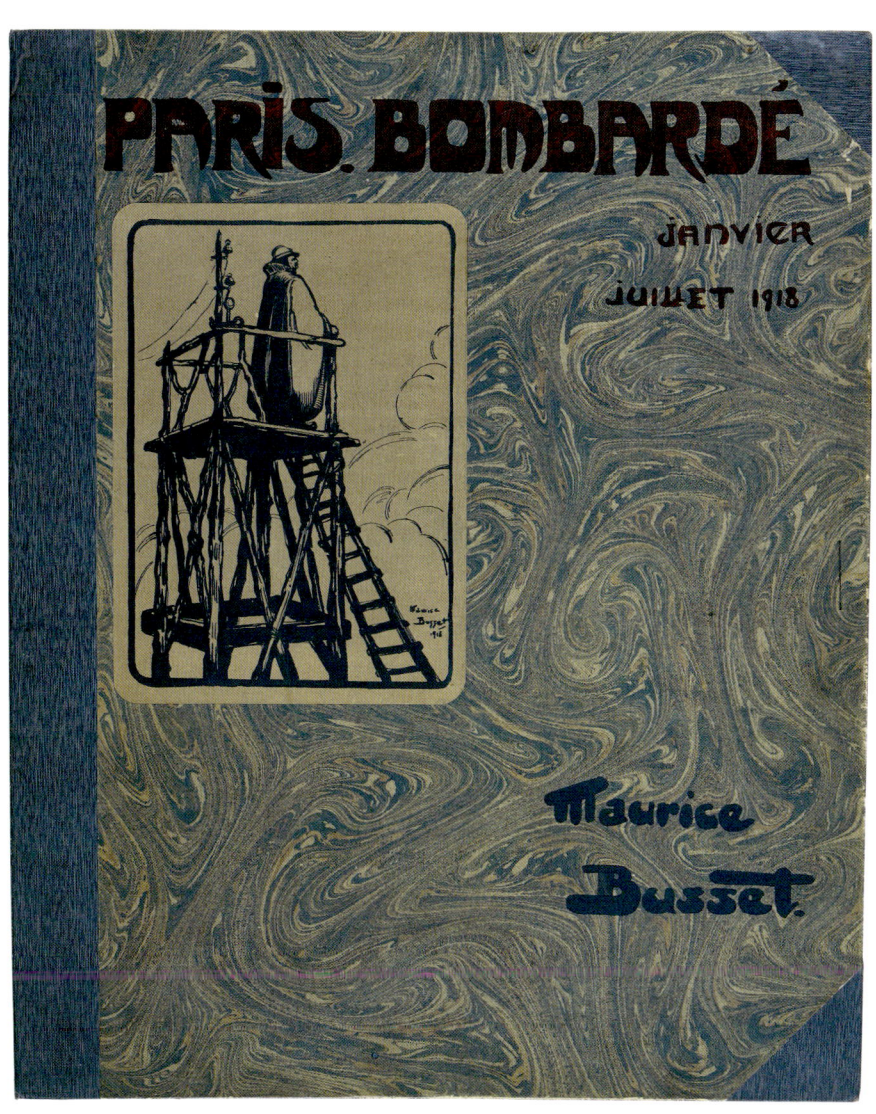

I
Maurice Busset, *Combat sur les nuages* (Combat above the Clouds), 1918

II
Maurice Busset, *La poursuite d'un Taube* (The Pursuit of a Taube), 1918

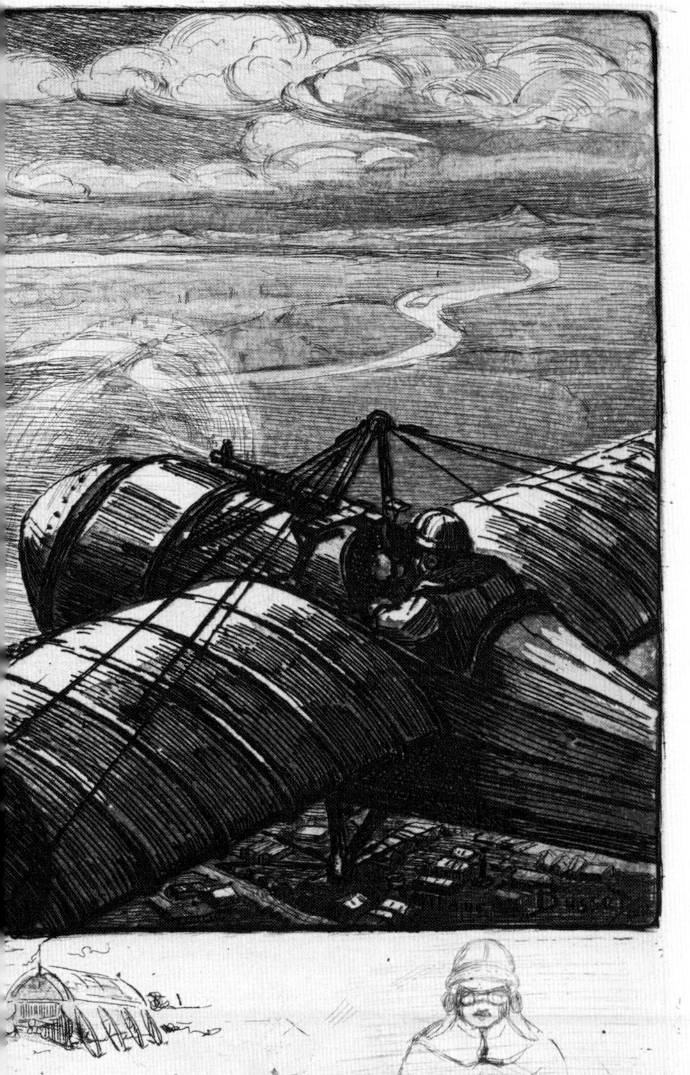

III
Maurice Busset, *Le guetteur* (The Watchman), 1918

IV
Maurice Busset, *La sirène de Notre-Dame* (The Siren of Notre Dame), 1918

V
Maurice Busset, *Les Gothas* (The Gothas), 1918

VI
Maurice Busset, *Les projecteurs, Paris vu du fort de Châtillon*
(The Searchlights, Paris Seen from the Fort de Châtillon), 1918

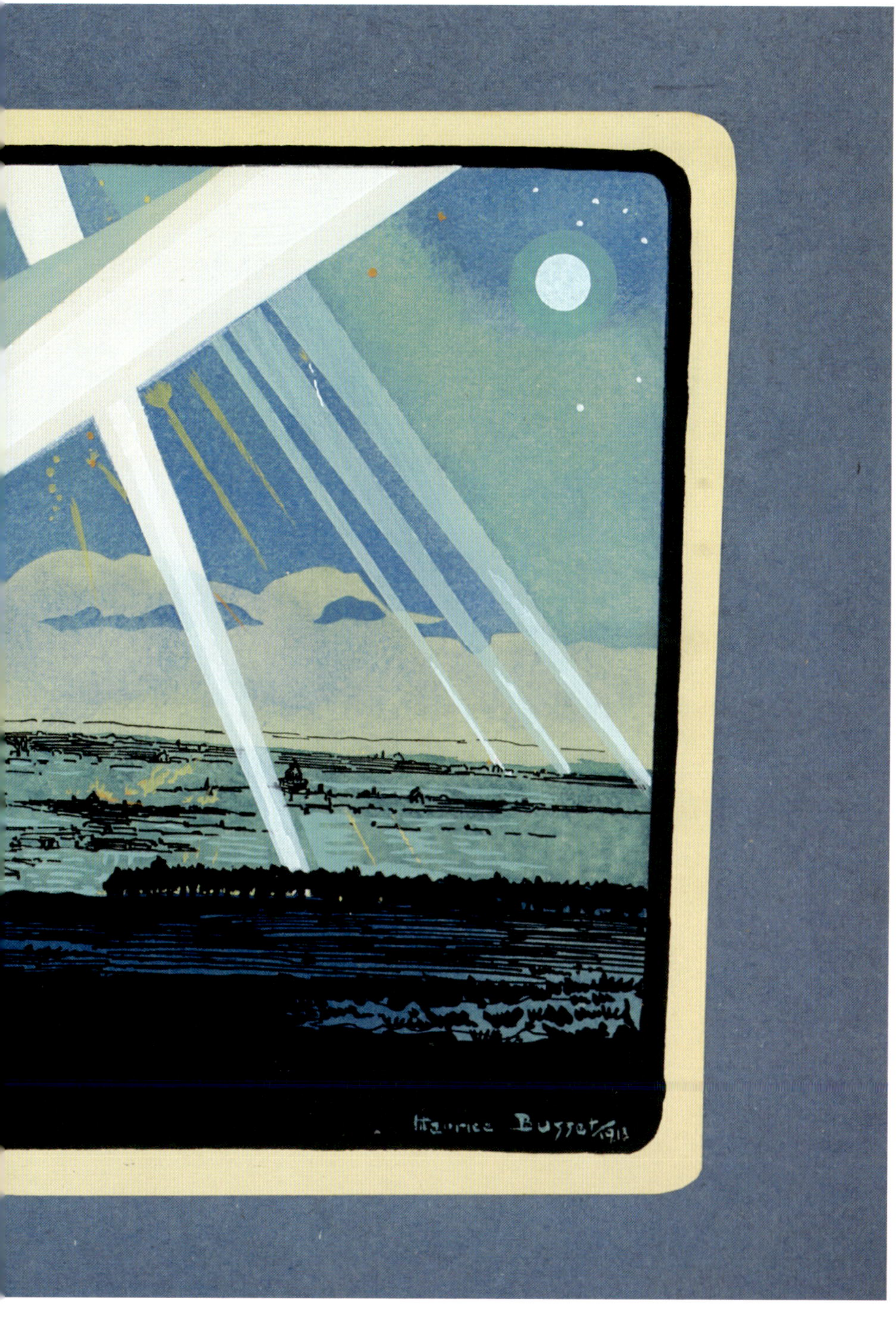
Maurice Busset

VII
Maurice Busset, *Parisiens se rendant aux abris souterrains*
(Parisians Rushing into Underground Shelters), 1918

VIII
Maurice Busset, *Avion-canon de la défense en vol sur la cité*
(Armed Defense Airplane in Flight over the City), 1918

IX
Maurice Busset, *Sous les voutes du métro Odéon, 27 Juin 1918*
(Under the Vaults of the Odéon Métro Station, June 27, 1918), 1918

X
Maurice Busset, *Péniches incendiées sous Notre-Dame, nuit du 21 Juin 1918*
(Burning Barges below Notre Dame, Night of June 21, 1918), 1918

XI
Maurice Busset, *L'Explosion de la rue de Rivoli vue du Pont-Marie*
(The Explosion on the Rue de Rivoli Seen from the Pont-Marie), 1918

XII
Maurice Busset, *Rue de Rivoli, la nuit du 11 Avril 1918*
(Rue de Rivoli, the Night of April 11, 1918), 1918

XIII
Maurice Busset, *La saucisse du Luxembourg*
(The Observation Balloon of Luxembourg Gardens), 1919

XIV
Maurice Busset, *Auto-canon au pied de l'éléphant du bassin du Trocadéro* (Automobile-mounted Cannon at the Foot of the Elephant of the Trocadero Basin), 1919

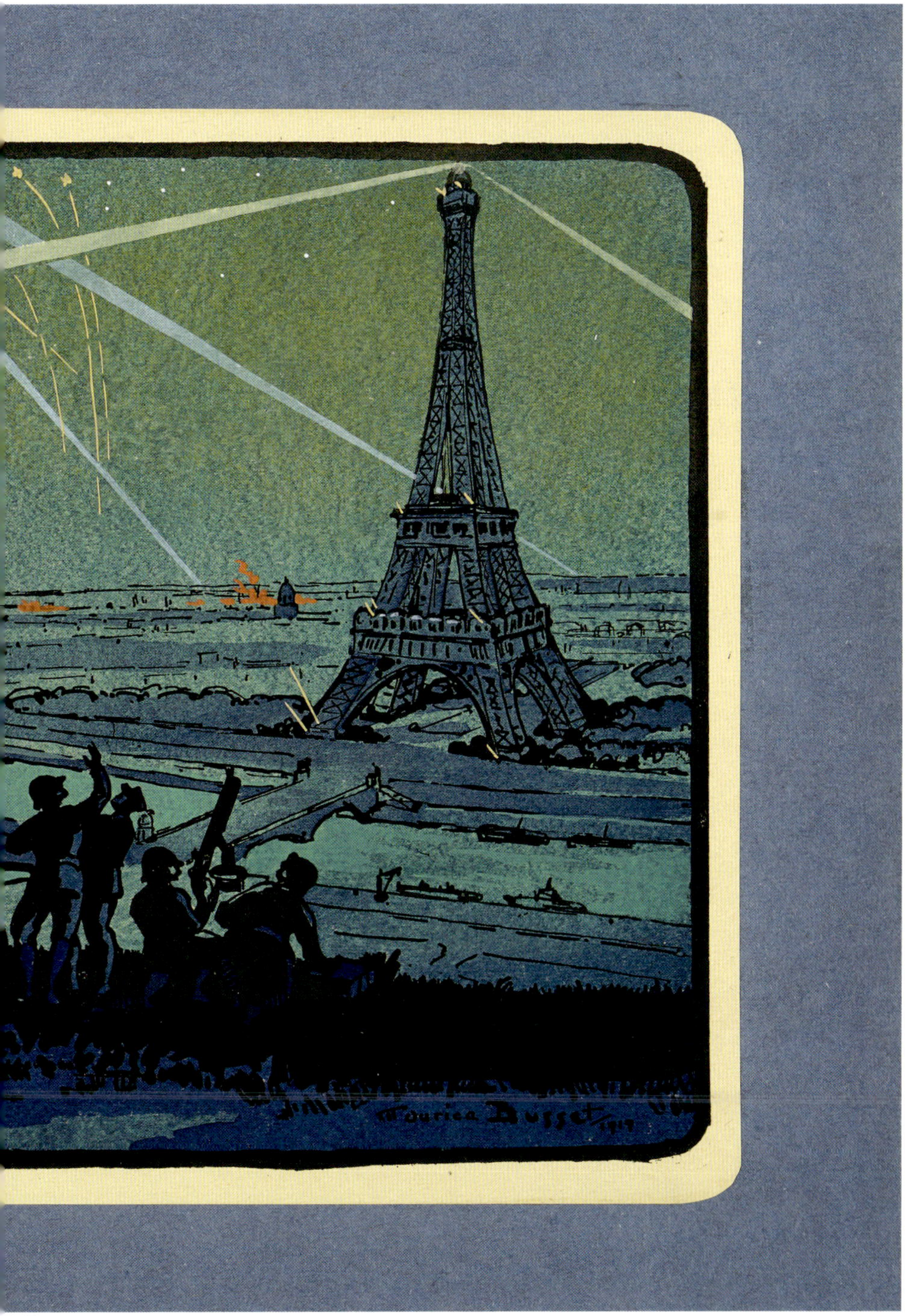
Maurice Busset 1917

XV
Maurice Busset, *La bombe de 100 kg de la rue Geoffroy-Marie*
(The 100 kg Bomb on the Rue Geoffroy-Marie), 1918

PLATES

XVI
Ludwig Hesshaimer, *Und über Mensch Tier und Erd in namenlosem Grausen, Apokalypsenreiter richtend Brausen* (And over Man and Beast and Earth, Apocalypse Horsemen Spread Unspeakable Horrors), 1921

XVII
Ludwig Hesshaimer, *Die Geister der Maschinen hat der Tod befreit / Mit grauser Wonne jeder Stahl und Feuer speit* (Death Has Freed the Spirits of the Machines / Each Spitting Steel and Fire with Horrible Delight), 1921

MIT GRAUSER WONNE JEDER STAHL UND FEUER SPEIT.

XVIII
C. R. W. Nevinson, *Assembling Parts*, 1917

XIX
C. R. W. Nevinson, *Making the Engine*, 1917

XX
C. R. W. Nevinson, *Acetylene Welding*, 1917

XXI
C. R. W. Nevinson, *Swooping Down on a Taube*, 1917

XXII
C. R. W. Nevinson, *Banking at 4,000 Feet*, 1917

XXIII
C. R. W. Nevinson, *In the Air*, 1917

XXIV
André Devambez, *Les trous d'obus* (The Shell Holes), c. 1917

XXV
Anselmo Bucci, *In volo sulle linee: Da cielo da terra* (In Flight over the Lines: From Sky to Earth), 1918

XXVI
Adolfo De Carolis, *Ignoto militi* (To the Unknown Soldier), c. 1922

XXVII
Monte Cevedale—La lotta sui ghiacciai (Monte Cevedale—The Battle on the Glaciers), c. 1917

XXVIII
Palmanova, c. 1917

71

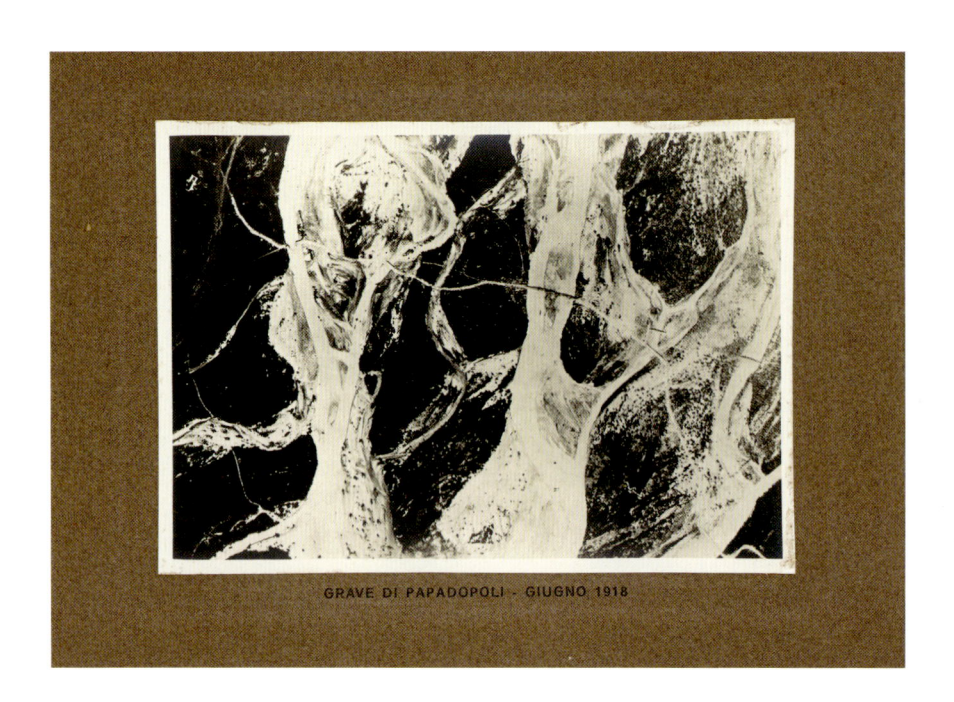

XXIX
Grave di Papadopoli—Giugno 1918, c. 1917
XXX
Monte Grappa—Le trincee dell'Asolone (Mount Grappa—The Trenches of Asolone), c. 1917

XXXI
Lieutenant Costantino Cattoi, *Asiago dopo l'incendio* (Asiago after the Fire), c. 1917

XXXII
Lieutenant Costantino Cattoi, *Bombardamento del Monte Zebio* (Bombardment of Mount Zebio), c. 1917
XXXIII
Un ponte sul Piave (A Bridge over the Piave), c. 1917

XXXIV
Flyer dropped by squadron of Italian aircraft over Vienna, 1918

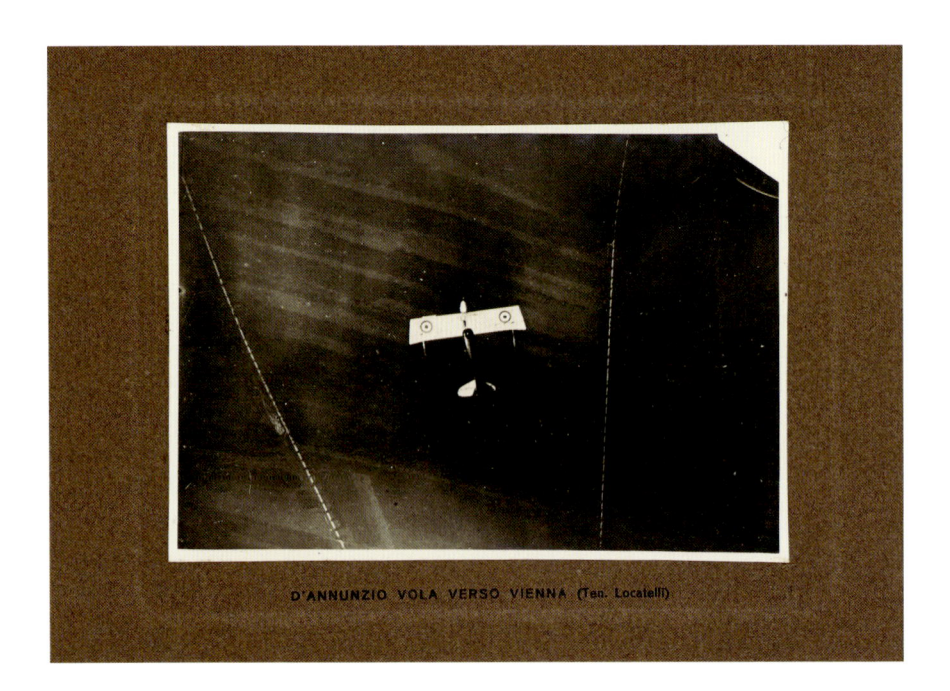

XXXV
Lieutenant Antonio Locatelli, *D'Annunzio vola verso Vienna* (D'Annunzio Flies towards Vienna), 1918
XXXVI
La sentenza cade su Vienna (The Judgment Falls on Vienna), 1918

ADOLPHE PÉGOUD.

« Le 5 février 1915 a attaqué à bonne distance un monoplan et en provoqua la chute. Presque immédiatement après, il put attaquer deux biplans successivement, provoqua la chute du premier et força le second à l'atterrissage. »
A été tué dans un glorieux combat, le 31 août 1915.
(*Citation à l'ordre du jour de l'armée*.)

XXXVII
Robert Bonfils, *Adolphe Pégoud*, 1918

XXXVIII
Victor-Emile Descaves, *Navarre*, 1917

XXXIX
Victor-Emile Descaves, *Nungesser*, 1917

XL
Victor-Emile Descaves, *Guynemer*, 1917

80

XLI
Victor-Emile Descaves, *Heurteaux*, 1917

XLII
Victor-Emile Descaves, *Dorme*, 1917

82

XLIII
János Kugler, *A levegó hóse* (Hero of the Air), 1914–18

XLIV
Julius E. F. Gipkens, *Gebt! Helft unsern tapfern Luftfahrern*
(Give! Help Our Brave Aviators), c. 1915

XLV
Julius E. F. Gipkens, *Helft! Helft unsern heldenmütigen Luftfahrern* (Help! Help Our Heroic Aviators), c. 1915

XLVI
Fritz Preiss, *Richthofen*, 1918

XLVII
Wilhelm Adolph Wellner, *Richthofen*, 1918

XLVIII
Maurice Busset, *Attaque d'une saucisse—le parachute*
(Attack on an Observation Balloon—The Parachute), c. 1919

IMAGE CAPTIONS

All works from The Wolfsonian–FIU, The Mitchell Wolfson, Jr. Collection, unless otherwise noted.

The Art of Aerial Warfare

Fig. 1
Photograph, *Women Welding Water Jackets on Liberty Engine Cylinders*, c. 1917
From *Cadillac Participation in the World War*, p. 46
Cadillac Motor Car Company, Detroit, publisher
3 7/8 x 6 1/2 in. (9.8 x 16.5 cm)
XB1990.1200

Fig. 2
Photograph, *Cima Dodici*, 1917
From *L'Illustrazione Italiana*, Vol. 64, No. 24 (June 17, 1917), p. 507
Milan
12 1/8 x 9 in. (30.8 x 22.9 cm)
XB2014.08.8.6

Fig. 3
Detail, Plate XXX
Photograph, *Monte Grappa–Le trincee dell'Asolone* (Mount Grappa–The Trenches of Asolone), c. 1917
From the album *Visione alata della guerra d'Italia* (Winged Vision of the War in Italy), c. 1922
Lieutenant Costantino Cattoi (Italian, 1894–1975), editor
Edizioni d'Arte del Cav. Astro Prosdocimi, Rome, publisher
10 x 14 in. (25 x 36 cm)
86.2.268

Fig. 4
Periodical cover, L'*Illustrazione Italiana*, Vol. 45, No. 33, 1918
Giovanni Cividini (Italian, 1879–1959), photographer
Milan
16 x 11 1/2 in. (40.6 x 29.2 cm)
XB2014.08.8.9

Fig. 5
Illustration, *Il tragico eroico volo del Capitano Salomone* (The Tragic Heroic Flight of Captain Salomone), 1916
Giuseppe Palanti (Italian, 1881–1946), illustrator
From *L'Illustrazione Italiana*, Vol. 43, No. 10 (March 5, 1916), p. 191
Milan
12 5/8 x 8 3/4 in. (32 x 22.2 cm)
XB2014.08.8.4

Fig. 6
Periodical cover, *Wachtfeuer* (Watch Fire), No. 136, 1917
W. Jordan, illustrator
Berlin
8 x 5 1/4 in. (20.3 x 13.3 cm)
XC1992.34.6

Fig. 7
Periodical cover, *Wachtfeuer* (Watch Fire), No. 175, 1918
W. Jordan, illustrator
Berlin
8 x 5 1/4 in. (20.3 x 13.3 cm)
XC1992.34.6

Maurice Busset's Modernity: The Prints of *Paris bombardé*

Fig. 1
Photograph, *Les bombardements aériens de Paris en 1918* (The Aerial Bombardments of Paris in 1918), 1918
Branger and Meurisse, photographers
From *L'Illustration*, Paris, January 1919, Vol. 77

Fig. 2
Photograph, *Parigi: La sala di un asilo infantile colpita dal cannone tedesco che bombarda la città* (Paris: The Room of a Kindergarten Struck by German Cannons that Bombarded the City), c. 1918
From *L'Illustrazione Italiana*, May 5, 1918, Vol. 45, No. 18, p. 360
Milan
16 x 11 1/2 in. (40.6 x 29.2 cm)
XB2014.08.8.8

Fig. 3
Print, *L'Héroisme des soldats de l'air* (The Heroism of the Soldiers in the Air), c. 1919
Maurice Busset (French, 1879–1936)
From the portfolio, *En avion: vols et combats* (In an Airplane: Flights and Fights)
Librairie Delgrave, Paris, publisher
13 x 20 in. (33 x 51 cm)
XB1992.960

91

PLATES I–XV

Portfolio, *Paris bombardé*, c. 1919
Maurice Busset (French, 1879–1936)
Blondel La Rougery, Paris, publisher
Plates: 10 ½ x 15 in. (26.6 x 38 cm)
The Wolfsonian–FIU, The Mitchell Wolfson, Jr. Collection of Decorative and Propaganda Arts, Promised Gift, MP2013.70.4

I
Combat sur les nuages
(Combat above the Clouds)
Etching

II
La poursuite d'un Taube
(The Pursuit of a Taube)
Etching

III
Le guetteur (The Watchman)
Woodcut

IV
La Sirène de Notre-Dame
(The Siren of Notre Dame)
Woodcut

V
Les Gothas (The Gothas)
Woodcut

VI
Les projecteurs, Paris vu du fort de Châtillon (The Searchlights, Paris Seen from the Fort de Châtillon)
Woodcut

VII
Parisiens se rendant aux abris souterrains (Parisians Rushing into Underground Shelters)
Woodcut

VIII
Avion canon de la défense en vol sur la cité (Armed Defense Airplane in Flight over the City)
Woodcut

IX
Sous les voutes du métro Odéon, 27 Juin 1918 (Under the Vaults of the Odéon Metro Station, June 27, 1918)
Woodcut

X
Péniches incendiées sous Notre-Dame, nuit du 21 Juin 1918 (Burning Barges below Notre Dame, Night of June 21, 1918)
Woodcut

XI
L'Explosion de la rue de Rivoli vue du Pont-Marie (The Explosion on the Rue de Rivoli Seen from the Pont-Marie)
Woodcut

XII
Rue de Rivoli, la nuit du 11 Avril 1918 (Rue de Rivoli, Night of April 11, 1918)
Woodcut

XIII
La saucisse du Luxembourg
(The Observation Balloon of Luxembourg Gardens)
Woodcut

XIV
Auto-canon au pied de L'éléphant du bassin du Trocadéro (Automobile-mounted Cannon at the Foot of the Elephant of the Trocadero Basin)
Woodcut

XV
La bombe de 100 kg de la rue Geoffroy-Marie (The 100 kg Bomb on the Rue Geoffroy-Marie)
Woodcut

PLATES XVI–XVII

Portfolio, *Die Weltkrieg: Ein Totentanz*
(The World War: A Dance of Death), 1921
Ludwig Hesshaimer
(Austrian, 1872–1956)
Wiener Literarische Anstalt, Vienna,
publisher
Christoph Reisser's Söhne, Vienna, printer
Etchings
Plates: 24 x 19 in. (61 x 48.3 cm)
TD1992.49.2.10–11

XVI

*Und über Mensch Tier und Erd in
namenlosem Grausen, Apokalypsenreiter
richtend Brausen* (And over Man and
Beast and Earth, Apocalypse Horsemen
Spread Unspeakable Horrors)

XVII

*Die Geister der Maschinen hat der Tod
befreit / Mit grauser Wonne jeder Stahl
und Feuer speit* (Death Has Freed the
Spirits of the Machines / Each Spitting
Steel and Fire with Horrible Delight)

PLATES XVIII–XXIII

Portfolio, *Building Aircraft*, 1918
C. R. W. Nevinson (British, 1889–1946)
Ministry of Information, His Majesty's
Stationary Office, London, publisher
Lithographs
Plates: 20 1/8 x 15 1/4 in. (51.1 x 38.6 cm)
85.4.64.43–48

XVIII
Assembling Parts, 1917

XIX
Making the Engine, 1917

XX
Acetylene Welding, 1917

XXI
Swooping Down on a Taube, 1917

XXII
Banking at 4,000 Feet, 1917

XXIII
In the Air, 1917

PLATE XXIV

Print, *Les trous d'obus* (The Shell Holes),
c. 1917
André Devambez (French, 1867–1944)
From the portfolio *Douze eaux-fortes*
(Twelve Etchings)
France
Etching
20 x 15 ¾ in. (51 x 40 cm)
XC2013.03.3

PLATE XXV

Print, *In volo sulle linee: Da cielo da terra*
(In Flight over the Lines: From Sky to
Earth), 1918
Anselmo Bucci (Italian, 1887–1955)
From the portfolio *Marina a terra: Schizzi
e disegni del soldato Anselmo Bucci* (Naval
Infantry: Sketches and Drawings by
the Soldier Anselmo Bucci), plate XXXIV
Ufficio Speciale del Ministero della
Marina, publisher
Alfieri & Lacroix, Milan, printer
18 ½ x 13 ¾ in. (47 x 35 cm)
83.2.533

PLATES XXVI–XXXVI

Album, *Visione alata della guerra d'Italia*
(Winged Vision of the War in Italy), c. 1922
Lieutenant Costantino Cattoi
(Italian, 1894–1975), editor
Edizioni d'Arte del Cav. Astro Prosdocimi,
Rome, publisher
Plates: 10 x 14 in. (25 x 36 cm),
unless otherwise noted
86.2.268

XXVI

Ignoto militi (To the Unknown Soldier),
c. 1922
Adolfo De Carolis (Italian, 1874–1928)
Wood engraving
13 ¾ x 9 ½ in. (34.9 x 23.8 cm)

XXVII

Monte Cevedale—La lotta sui ghiacciai
(Monte Cevedale—The Battle on the
Glaciers), c. 1917

XXVIII

Palmanova, c. 1917

XXIX

Grave di Papadopoli—Giugno 1918, 1918

XXX

Monte Grappa—Le trincee dell'Asolone (Mount Grappa—The Trenches of Asolone), c. 1917

XXXI

Asiago dopo l'incendio (Asiago after the Fire), c. 1917
Lieutenant Costantino Cattoi (Italian, 1894–1975), photographer

XXXII

Bombardamento del Monte Zebio (Bombardment of Mount Zebio), c. 1917
Lieutenant Costantino Cattoi (Italian, 1894–1975), photographer

XXXIII

Un ponte sul Piave (A Bridge over the Piave), c. 1917

XXXIV

Flyer dropped by squadron of Italian aircraft over Vienna, 1918

XXXV

D'Annunzio vola verso Vienna (D'Annunzio Flies towards Vienna), 1918
Lieutenant Antonio Locatelli (Italian, 1895–1936), photographer

XXXVI

La sentenza cade su Vienna (The Judgment Falls on Vienna), 1918

PLATE XXXVII

Print, *Adolphe Pégoud*, 1918
Robert Bonfils (French, 1886–1972)
From the portfolio *La manière Française* (The French Way)
Lutetia, Paris, printer
12 ⅝ x 9 ⅜ in. (32.4 x 24.2 cm)
The Wolfsonian–FIU, The Mitchell Wolfson, Jr. Collection of Decorative and Propaganda Arts, Promised Gift, WC2005.3.1.3

PLATES XXXVIII–XLII

Portfolio, *Quelques as Français* (Several French Flying Aces), 1917
Victor-Emile Descaves
(French, 1899–1959)
Le Nouvel Essor, Paris, publisher
Woodcuts
Plates: 13 x 9 ⅛ in. (33.4 x 23.8 cm)
The Wolfsonian–FIU, The Mitchell Wolfson, Jr. Collection of Decorative and Propaganda Arts, Promised Gift, WC2005.1.6.38

XXXVIII
Navarre

XXXIX
Nungesser

XL
Guynemer

XLI
Heurteaux

XLII
Dorme

PLATE XLIII

Photograph, *A levegő hőse* (Hero of the Air), 1914–18
János Kugler (Hungarian), photographer
From the album *Az Érdekes Újság Háborus albuma*–II. füzet (The Interesting News War Album–Issue II)
Otto Légrády et al., Budapest, publisher
14 ⅛ x 11 ¼ in. (35.9 x 28.6 cm)
The Wolfsonian–FIU, The Mitchell Wolfson, Jr. Collection of Decorative and Propaganda Arts, Promised Gift, T2014.67.4

PLATE XLIV

Poster, *Gebt! Helft unsern tapfern Luftfahrern* (Give! Help Our Brave Aviators), c. 1915
Julius E. F. Gipkens
(German, 1883–1968), designer
Hollerbaum & Schmidt, Berlin, printer
Offset lithograph
56 ¼ x 75 in. (142.9 x 190.6 cm)
TD1991.31.3 a,b

PLATE XLV

Poster, *Helft! Helft unsern heldenmütigen Luftfahrern* (Help! Help Our Heroic Aviators), c. 1915

Julius E. F. Gipkens (German, 1883–1968), designer

Hollerbaum & Schmidt, Berlin, printer

Offset Lithograph

56 ¼ x 75 in. (142.9 x 190.6 cm)

TD1991.31.2 a,b

PLATE XLVI

Periodical cover, *Wachtfeuer* (Watch Fire), No. 187, 1918

Fritz Preiss (German, b. 1883), illustrator

Berlin

8 x 5 ¼ in. (20.3 x 13.3 cm)

XC1992.34.6

PLATE XLVII

Illustration, *Richthofen*, 1918

Wilhelm Adolph Wellner (German, 1859–1939), illustrator

From the periodical *Lustige Blätter* (Funny Pages), Vol. 33, No. 18, p. 3

Berlin

7 ¾ x 8 in. (19.7 x 20.3 cm)

TD1990.273.1

PLATE XLVIII

Print, *Attaque d'une saucisse—le parachute* (Attack on an Observation Balloon—The Parachute), c. 1919

Maurice Busset (French, 1879–1936)

From the portfolio *En avion: vols et combats* (In an Airplane: Flights and Fights)

Librairie Delgrave, Paris, publisher

20 x 13 in. (51 x 33 cm)

XB1992.960